GIVE HIM THANKS AND PRAISE

My Encounter with God

Theophilus Ugbedeojo Ejeh

GIVE HIM THANKS AND PRAISE

My Encounter with God

Bibliografische Information
der Deutschen Nationalbibliothek
Die Deutsche Nationalbibliothek verzeichnet diese
Publikation in der Deutschen Nationalbibliografie;
detaillierte bibliografische Daten sind im Internet
über www.dnb.de abrufbar.

Publisher's Note:
Comments, inquiries, and other
correspondences should be directed to:
Fr. Dr. Theophilus Ugbedeojo Ejeh.
E-mail Address: ugbedeojo@web.de

Herstellung und Verlag:
BoD – Books on Demand,
Norderstedt

ISBN: 978-3-7448-0952-8

"Come, let us praise the Lord! Let us sing for joy to God, who protects us! Let us come before him with thanksgiving and sing joyful songs of praise!"
(Ps. 95:1-2).

DEDICATION

To my parents:
late chief Patrick Ejeh & Mrs. Janet Ejeh and
to all my Beloved ones who have always encouraged
me to give thanks and praise to God.

PREFACE

Mother Theresa of Calcutta often admonished her sisters to "go to work on a smile". This practice is, perhaps informed by the popular belief that SMILE, like honey attracts more ‚clients‘ to the Lord when one is on the master's business than does a lugubrious, gloomy face, which ostensibly repels would-be clients of the kingdom like vinegar. It is probably with such a backdrop that the author of "GIVE HIM THANKS AND PRAISE", Rev. Fr. Ugbedeojo Theophilus Ejeh generously shares his own personal encounter with God with his audience. I have personally known the author over the years as one who lives in an atmosphere of praise and endeavours to spread the fragrance of the Lord's presence. His experience seems to portray most vividly that the more one spreads this ‚perfume‘ of thanksgiving and praise in one's life, no matter what odds one is faced with, the more contagious the ‚magic‘ of genuine conversion becomes. As a matter of fact, praise is pictured as a strong key to God's treasure house. In this beautiful and inspiring piece, the author strives to unlock the door to the secret of an enduring happiness, sustained victory, eternal success, radiant glory, indormitable power, divine wisdom, all embracing love, integral healing, undaunting courage, unflagging zeal, undying fervour and above all, abiding peace. The work is made up of five simple chapters. Chapter one discusses the nature and power in thanksgiving. Chapter two shows how in praise, God is acknowledged as God. This, according to the writer, puts smile on God's face, keeps his people awake, strengthens them and brings about miracles on its wings. In chapter three, he shares his entire life story in the light of one-big-praise testimony. In chapter four he tries to convince the reader on why God deserves our praise and thanksgiving in all situations. Even over what we might consider as thorny problems, snailish answers to or rocket answers to prayers, God is to be praised. For He is God of all wisdom. Chapter five dwells on conditions, or rather, dispositions for thanksgiving. Here, there is a serious stress on humility, selflessness, fear of God, faithfulness, contentment, self abandonment, total reliance on divine providence and optimism. In a world ridden with so much pessimism, the author of GIVE HIM THANKS AND PRAISE offers us a thorough-going manner of facing life with great optimism. He goes further to show the reader that an ingrate is the most unfortunate of fellows. This book would therefore teach you how to be eternally grateful not only to fellow humans who have done you some favour but more so, to God who is the author of life itself.

Rev. Fr. Fidelis Eleojo Egbunu (Ph.D.)

ACKNOWLEDGEMENTS

I am first and foremost grateful to God who has called me to serve and to praise Him; I am also grateful to the Blessed Virgin Mary for her intercessions. I will not, at this juncture, fail to sincerely acknowledge the effort of my late bishop Most Rev. E. S. Obot in training me both at home and abroad to become a priest of the Most High God and for giving the approval for me to be ordained and thereby daily offer the greatest sacrifice of thanksgiving and praise which is the Holy Eucharist. My thanks go further to my present bishop Most Rev. Anthony A. Adaji for his care and support. I will not fail to express my heart felt thanks to Very Rev. Fr. Dr. Fidelis Eleojo Egbunu for his brotherly support, particularly in reading through this booklet and correcting it and for accepting to write the preface to it. Many thanks to Dr. Fritz Krappe for corrections made and also to Fr. Dr. Innocent Oyibo for taking his time to go through the work and giving his personal comment on it. Thanks particularly to Mr. Herbert Kantus and Sergio Leone for their technical support. I remain indebted to all my beloved ones who in one way or the other assisted me to publish the second edition of this booklet; may the Almighty God bless and reward them in hundred folds.

Theophilus Ugbedeojo Ejeh

INTRODUCTION

My flair for thanksgiving and praise actually surfaced during my free Semester in a town in Germany called Münster. I was fortunate to be living in a seminary where this was encouraged. The Seminarians there usually have a spiritual theme for each semester; the theme for that particular semester (winter semester of 2000/2001) was on the principle of praise. This was to nurture them through that period. Talks were given on it severally; the spiritual director, in particular, emphasised the singing of praises on daily basis. He told us that we could even sing joyfully, chanting praises as we wake up from sleep and go into the bathroom and this will carry us through the day, since the first mood one has in the morning will determine what mood one will have the whole of the day. It was in this „praise encouraged atmosphere" that I, at the point of waking up one morning (still not quite conscious), had the following words on my lips: "Lass die ganze Erde erkennen, dass der Herr Gott ist" (German) – "Let the whole earth know that the Lord is God". I was still learning how to speak German then, and so had to ascertain the correctness of the sentence from one of the German seminarians around. He eventually confrmed it. And checking it up later in the Bible, I discovered that these words are contained in 1Kg. 8:60. My desire to write on thanksgiving and praise originally started at this point. I thus looked forward to share my experience of praise and thanksgiving with others, especially the great joy that is involved in it.

I was once asked by a German friend about what I will like to do when I go back home to Nigeria. My response was that I would like to bring to everybody's awareness, particularly the young people, the importance of singing praises to God. This dream is gradually coming true in this booklet. It is my great desire for all who will read it to encounter the great joy and power that ensue from the thanksgiving and praise principle. What I mean here is not just what we do in the church alone, but that which is constant, either in the church or outside the church, either loud or silent, deep down our being and with our whole life (cf. Ps. 103: 1-2). This is the transforming thanksgiving and praise which I want to encourage everyone to get used to. I believe that this piece shall transform so many souls that will come in contact with it. We shall first of all throw some light on the meaning of thanksgiving, its nature, power and fruits, and thereafter, go over to defining the concept of praise, its connection to thanksgiving and benefits and then to my personal encounters, which will lead us into seeing the reasons for thanksgiving and praise in our lives and finally to the necessary conditions needed to practise the principle of thanksgiving and praise. In the appendix are some Praise Psalms and hymns and personally composed prayers which may help us.

Fr. Theophilus Ugbedeojo Ejeh

TABLE OF CONTENT

Chapter 1:

Chapter 2:

Chapter 3:

CHAPTER 1:

1.1   Thanksgiving Defined

Thanksgiving according to Hermann Bezzel is the greatest power of our life; and according to a Zairian thought, it is just "... to sit oneself before God and to rejoice" (cf. Dziewas, D., 2000). Thanksgiving is what we do daily to our fellow human beings when we experience love or care from them. The amazing thing is that we thank our neighbours most often when they help us, but find it hard to thank God most times from our hearts, probably because we do not see Him physically. Worst of all, we concentrate so much on our problems without counting our blessings which could come from another angle of our lives just as Helen Keller rightly expressed as quoted ,by Fr. Fidelis C. B. Kwazu in his book „How To Carry Your Cross": „When one door of happiness closes another one opens; but we look so long at the closed door that we do not see the one which has been opened for us." If we should open our eyes widely, we shall see the hand of God at work in our lives and would have the cause to thank Him at all times as an expression of our gratitude. Thanksgiving is the greatest service we can render to God which is quite pleasing to Him (cf. Ps. 50:14;23). Martin Luther in light of this says: „We cannot do any greater work for God or any service rendering except to thank Him" (cf. Dziewas, 2000). Norman Vincent Peale, the great author of "Power of Positive Thinking" says the following about thanksgiving in his book "How to be your best": "Thanksgiving is one of the most important, most creative capacities of the human mind. As we practice it, assiduously and constantly, we develop a deep joy in living, even though life is filled with all manner of suffering and difficulty. The individual who learns to practice thanksgiving activates within himself, and around himself, continuous victories and blessings from God. If you practice thanksgiving, victory, and joy, and satisfaction will be engendered in your life, and will contribute to the happiness of all those who touch your life".

1.2   The Nature of Thanksgiving

Thanksgiving is a humble activity; humility is what God requires from us. David said in this regard: „A humble contrite heart, Lord, you will not scorn" (PS.51:17); that is to say that the Lord finds favour with the humble heart and he who gives thanks has a humble heart, and he finds more favour from the person to whom the thanks is given. A German proverb says: „A man goes through the town safely, without a problem, with his hat in his hands". It is an act of humility to remove one's cap at the moment one meets his elders and bending down to greet them. The young man who practises this receives great blessings from the elders. In like manner, the one who says thanks for the help received creates the way for many more blessings. For those of us who are catholics, the core of thanksgiving in our worship is the Holy Mass which is termed the „Holy Eucharist" from the Greek origin „eucharistia" meaning „thanksgiving". It is against this backdrop that F. E. Egbunu in his book „Get Your Prayers Answered By Praying In The Spirit" thus says: "The celebration of the Eucharstic Banquet is at the peak of all thanksgiving and praises to God. For by so doing we offer the perfect sacrifice."

1.3   The Power of Thanksgiving

A story is told of' two angels who came from heaven each day to collect the people's petitions and thanksgivings for God. One collected the petitions and the other the thanksgivings. At the end of each day, the angel with the basket for the petitions had his filled to the brim, while the one with the basket for the thanksgivings went back with just one or two thanksgivings. Many do not realise the power in giving thanks and so do not care much about it. Thanksgiving in itself heals, it is an expression that we really know the importance of what we have received. When we, for example, give thanks to God for the gift of our lives, our eyes are opened to see many more wonders the Lord has done for us. It is in view of this that Liselotte Nold describes thanksgiving as „... the key to the treasure of our life." We discover more of God's providence in our lives when we give thanks. This leads us into unceasing praises. We become happy and are able to give a share of this happiness further to other people and in this way fulfil the purpose for which God has made us, namely to love and serve Him and our neighbour by the fruits of the joy we bear. Jesus asked the man whom He healed among the ten lepers, and who came back to thank Him: „Ten were cleansed, were they not? Where are the other nine?" (Lk. 17:17). It is a sign of courtesy to at least say „thanks". We know how we wait for people to say „thanks" for what we give to them or for what we did for them. Thanksgiving makes the one, who carried out the good deed happy and gives him the room to do more. It is not as if God needs our thanks at all cost, our thanksgiving is a pleasing sacrifice to Him which also opens the door of our own heart to see and receive more of His blessings. It is thus expressed in the preface of Weekday IV of the Roman Missal „Our prayer of thanksgiving adds nothing to your greatness, but makes us grow in your grace". Thanksgiving, in this sense, can, therefore, be termed „a key" that opens the treasure of God's great blessings. He who possesses this key has the access to this great treasure at all times. Albert Schweitzer has rightly put it: „Anyone who thanks God from his heart will become rich in himself." We may be complaining that our prayers are not answered, but we have, probably, not opened our door with thanksgiving to receive what we need. Thanksgiving is a key that opens our pocket and heart to receive what we have prayed for. It is an expression of faith. We see this in Jesus in the manner He prays here: "I thank you, Father, that you listen to me. I know that you always listen to me, but I say this for the sake of the people here, so that they will believe that you sent me." After he said this, he called out in a loud voice, „Lazarus, come out!" He came out, his hands and feet wrapped in grave clothes and with a cloth round his face. „Untie him", Jesus told them, „and let him go" (Jn.11:41- 44). This is one of the many great wonders that Jesus worked. It was faith powered by thanksgiving that aided Jesus to do this miracle.

1.4 Thanksgiving Likened to the Attitude of Little Children

I once saw a child playing in his father's arms in the Cathedral Church of Münster in Germany and was excited by the whole scene. The small boy was so happy in the arms of his father that he did not even know what to do with him. He kissed his head several times, looked into his eyes severally and might have said to himself: „You are my father. I am happy to be in your arms and to have your arms around me." I try sometimes to imagine myself in the status of this child. Just like Philipp Keel once said: „Everyone should spare himself some minutes of being childlike in a day." The joy of being a child in the arms of a father is so great and indescribable. I remember how my father used to carry me as a small boy on his chest in the evenings. I felt so protected and happy playing there. I also try sometimes to project my relationship to Jesus in this way. I imagine Him holding me in His arms. Such thought helps me to grow in the act of thanksgiving and praise. The child who feels so secured in his father's arms is happy and grateful and so does a Christian who feels loved and protected by Jesus. Jesus admonishes His hearers to have the faith of little children: "Unless you change and become like little children, you will not inherit the kingdom of God" (Mt. 18:3). Children are always totally dependent on their parents. Our act of constant thanksgiving to God is an expression of our total dependency on Him. Jesus has told us that we can do nothing without Him (cf. Jn. 15:5). By our contant act of thanksgiving we tell Him that we cannot live without Him. By so doing we rely solely on God's power (cf. Zach. 4:6). Children have nothing on their own except that which they receive from their parents and other adults. They are grateful for the things they get, particularly from their parents and they believe that they will always receive from them whenever they are in need. A little child knows, for example, that his mother will carry him when he cries. He is very sure of the help he can get from his mother and father. This is the attitude our Lord demands from us. He wishes that we put all our trust in Him. How can this be possible? It is actually difficult, but there is something which unlocks this difficulty and lifts our hearts to God; it is thanksgiving and praise which open our hearts to trust in our loving Lord. Both do the wonder of transforming us into children through whose mouths the Lord is glorified (cf. Ps. 8:3).

The Lord is interested in our expression of dependency on Him and this we can do through the praises and the thanks we offer to Him, the fruit of our lips (cf. Heb. 13:15). Thanksgiving particularly does the wonder of leaving ourselves totally to God and trusting Him fully. It fills our hearts with the sweet presence of the Lord. It establishes a great bond between us and God. It transforms us into a pleasing instrument through which the Lord manifests his power.

1.5   It is Right to Give Thanks

Sometimes giving thanks to God becomes very easy for us and some other time difficult, that is when things begin to go bad. In moments of trial, our eyes are closed to the good things God had done for us and we complain like the Israelites, who, after God had delivered them from Egypt, were not grateful, for the fact that their enemies were still after them. They did not realise that God could still do much more for them at that moment. When we thank God, we affirm what he did for us in the past and express our belief in the fact that He can still do more for us. So, no matter what our problems may be, let us try to thank God at least for the gift of our life. There is a strength that comes along with the act of thanksgiving. It creates room for God to even do more for us. It opens us to the flow of God's blessings. The problem we think we have at the moment may block our view of the great blessings God has kept in store for us. When this happens, the enemy becomes happy. But once we are able to say: „God, I thank you for the gift of my life", the enemy becomes upset and gets away in shame. Then we will get the peace we long for, the blocked pipe of blessings will be opened and we find ourselves smiling. That is the wonder thanksgiving can do.

1.6. The Fruits of Thanksgiving

1.6.1 As Means of Winning Victory over Fear, Worry and Sin

A careful observation shows that many people are suffering under fears and worries. The act of constant thanksgiving sets us free from such problems and transforms us into healthy children of God, shielding us from physical and psychological ruins. It is in view of this that Gabriel Marcel thus says of thanksgiving as "… the protector of the soul against the powers of destruction". No wonder then Heinrich Janssen, an auxiliary bishop in Münster in Germany once said in a sermon that he who can no longer give thanks to God becomes bitter. Thanksgiving in itself transforms us and makes us whole and well. It sets us free from the atmosphere of sin. It gives us the energy to overcome sin, the energy flows naturally from God so long as we continue to thank and praise Him. "Let us, then, always offer praise to God as our sacrifice through Jesus, which is the offering presented by lips that confess Him as Lord" (Heb.13:15-16).

1.6.2 Thanksgiving as Expression of our Faith

When we have faith in something, we believe it actually exists. Thanksgiving is given to the person who is believed to be there or to exist. In this way, when we say „Thank you Lord" we are indirectly or rather directly thanking the Lord whom we believe to be there. When I thank God, I say yes to Him, I accept Him as someone who is there, and as someone whom I really need, someone who loves me so much and without whom I cannot live. I acknowledge Him as my Lord and creator through constant thanksgiving. When I, for example, say: „God, thank you for the gift of my life", I am in another way saying: „Thank you God for creating me." This in itself is an acknowledgement of my own existence and that of God. Through this, I come to also recognise the fact that my neighbour is a gift from God, God's own creature. I acknowledge him as a human person and I can then, for example, say „Thank you, Lord, for the gift of the life of my friend." I go further to see the whole of creation as God's gift, and this leads me into an unending thanksgiving. I now enjoy the world as God's own gift with thanksfulness and joy with an eye of faith. In this way we enjoy the world around us without having pessimistic view of it.

1.6.3   Thanksgiving as Means of Establishing Peace in Our Being

From my own experience, I have seen that the act of constant thanksgiving promotes and enhances peace in us. Many a time we discover that we are worried over so many things and need rest and peace in ourselves. Giving thanks to God at such a moment would make us to be calm and get our minds settled. St. Augustine has rightly put it that 'our hearts are restless until they rest in God.' The act of constant thanksgiving to God makes our minds to be focused on God the author of our being and the source of peace. In giving thanks to God, we breathe out all our worries, anxieties, fears, diseases, guilts, weaknesses etc. and take in the power of God. We need the strength of God to do our daily job in a way that will give glory to Him. Giving thanks to Him therefore helps us to attain this by making us calm in ourselves, recollected and focused. It helps us also to pray well and to relate well with people around us. When we give thanks we radiate joy and peace. Thanksgiving in this sense may be seen as an oil that lubricates our relationship with God and our neighbour. It is in view of this that Friedrich von Bodelschwingh says that life becomes lighter when one learns to say thanks for little things. The act of thanksgiving is something that is inevitable in the life of every human being. It is a practice that is highly recommended for our daily life. This can be done at all times in prayer and particularly in the act of praise.

"Thanksgiving is the key to the treasure of our life" (Liselotte Nold).

Chapter 2:

2.1   Praise Defined

Praise is an act of telling God that He is God. „It is a form of prayer which recognises most immediately that God is God" (CCC. 2639). It can also be seen as a form of approval or admiration of God. It is an expression of respect and gratitude as an act of worship. It has the old French origin „preisier" meaning „to price or praise", from Latin „premium" meaning „price" (cf. Oxford Compact English dictionary). I want to believe that the German form „preisen" meaning „to price or praise" must have also originated from the same root as the French.„To price something" means that we want to know the worth of that thing; this in a way explains what praising God means, which is to know the worth or rather the greatness of God and regarding it as such. We can praise a fellow human being for a wonderful job done, for a help rendered or for a kind gesture. It is the same thing we do when we express our gratitude to God or when we marvel at what He has done for us, just like in the New Testament where people praised God at wonders performed by Christ (cf. Mt. 8:27). Since praise can be seen as a form of showing gratitude, it can therefore also be seen as a form of thanksgiving. This is why their usage is almost synonymous. It is in view of this that Heinrich Janssen said that praise is always thanksgiving.

2.2   Praise As The Will Of God

All creation is meant to give glory to God. The Heaven serves God daily as it brings forth all the heavenly bodies. The sun, the moon and the stars do their own part in providing light. In this way, they give glory to God. What will happen, if the sun, the moon, and the stars are not functional? It is unimaginable! In the same way that these heavenly bodies serve God by doing what they are meant for, so also are we human beings created to serve the purpose of God, to praise Him and give Him glory and honour in our service. This is the source of our happiness and strength: to praise God. The will of God for us is very important. It is revealed to us in and through our Lord Jesus Christ who gave His life for our sake. This was the Father's purpose for Him, and in this was His crown and glory. God's will for us is to love Him with all our heart, soul and body and to love our neighbour as ourselves. When we love something we adore it, we praise it, it pleases us and we would never want to lose sight of it. If I love God, I want forever to be in His presence and to sing His praises, to glorify Him and to worship Him with songs. Just like the psalmist says: „One thing do I desire, to dwell in the house of the Lord all the days of my life" (Ps. 27:4). This love of being with God and of giving Him glory will further be transfered to my neighbour so long as I recognise the image of God in him. I make sure that this image of God in my neighbour is respected and preserved. I make sure that I have time also for my neighbour just like I have time for God. This is love!

It is our duty to sing praises to God at every moment of our lives. It is a major purpose for which we are created. The angels of God in Heaven sing praises to Him all the time. It is their duty to do it and the saints also join them in harmonizing the praises. And when we sing praises we join this heavenly community in giving glory to God. And our God who takes delight in our praises blesses us with His Spirit whenever we do so (cf. Ps. 22:3). Matthew E. Okenyi commenting on the need to praise God says: „It is the mind of God that man should for ever praise and worship Him in spirit and truth. God expects man to join the Cherubim, Seraphim, the 24 elders and enumerable (sic) angels of God to worship Him in the beauty of His holiness …" To participate in the act of praise therefore, is to take part in a great form of prayer which involves the angels and the saints. Let us give to God what belongs to Him; our praise is for Him. Let us give it to Him, for it is His due and it is our duty to do it. It is right to give thanks and praise to Him, for He does wonders for us even in the midst of troubles. In the Old Testament we are given the example of David who praised God greatly as he brought home the Ark of the Covenant. He danced to the extent that he became nacked and was mocked by one of his wives whom he later cursed (cf. 1Chr. 15:29). To show how much importance David attached to the singing of praises, we have the account of his choosing four thousand levites who were meant to be singing praises to God as their duty (cf. 1Chr. 23:5).

In the New Testament we are given the example of Paul and Silas who praised God so greatly that the prison shook and the gates were opened for them to go out (cf. Act.16: 25-26). They experienced victory like the Israelites did when they praised God and the Walls of Jericho fell down (cf. Josh 6:20). Praise therefore, is indispensable in our daily life and when we practise it, we fulfil God's will for us and we obtain the power we need for our daily life. Frances Metcalfe discovered the power in praise and put it thus:

"Praise unlocks, heaven's portals;
Praise causes doubts to cease;
Praise brings precious blessings;
Praise leaves the sweetest peace.
Praise breaks all bands asunder;
Praise sets the captives free;
Praise lightens every burden;
Praise is the master key.
Praise changes circumstances;
Praise establishes the heart;
When praise becomes perpetual,
Praise is a Holy Art."

2.3   Praise Makes God To Smile

I was once in the palace of the Atta1 of Igala with a host of Christians on the occasion of the concluding ceremony of the CAN (Christian Association of Nigeria) week of prayer. During our short visit there, I observed how somebody said a funny proverb before the Atta moved from his seat. It is something like .this: „Ich enwu ke kakini okuta i woji n, ba k´edu- edu r`ukpolo tinyo le" (Igala), meaning: „If you say: this stone is not heavy, that means you have thrown it away already." This is a kind of praise which so pleased the Atta. He smiled and got up to move away with more gusto. It so amused those of us around that we also smiled. This, I will say, is what happens whenever we praise God. God becomes so happy that he begins to smile and his smile spreads itself around us and brightens our faces. This smile also becomes contageous to others around us, such that a joyful atmosphere is created. Praise is as such a sacrifice that gives honour to God; this is why the psalmist would say: „Offer praise to God; fulfil your vows to the Most High. Then call on me in the time of distress; I will rescue you and you shall honour me. ...Understand this, you who forget God, lest I attack you with no one to rescue. Those who offer me praise as a sacrifice honour me; to the obedient I will show the salvation of God" (Ps. 50:14-15; 22-23).

2.4   Praise Keeps Us Awake In The Spirit

When I rely on my own power, I see myself falling. When I struggle on my own to keep fit in holiness, I see myself falling. Simon Peter was walking towards the Lord on the sea and when he recognised where he was, he tried to rely on his own power, at that point he began to sink into the water.

And the Lord asked him: „Why did you doubt, oh man of little faith?" (Mt. 14:31). When we put our faith in ourselves we begin to fear and sink into worries, sin, etc., but when we put our faith in the Lord we grow in holiness and strength. Many of us are suffering under the weight of our own flesh, we are struggling to bring it under control, but it remains difficult and despite that we still pretend that all is well. All is not well! That is a battle that remains as long as we are alive and active. This battle is not our battle (cf. 2 Chr. 20: 15-17). It belongs to the Lord and unless we go on our knees every now and then to tell the Lord and Master of our lives that the battle is not ours but His, we continue to fall again. We really need the humility to confess the fact that we cannot fight the battle ourselves. The Lord wants us to open our mouths to confess this fact before Him, we do not need to pretend to be little holy angels and go around thinking that all is under control. No, let us not pretend, let us confess to the Lord that we are made up of flesh and blood. Let us confess to the Lord that we need Him, that we need His power and His Spirit. The Lord himself says: „It is not by might, it is not by power but by my Spirit" (Zach.4:6). By His Spirit we shall conquer, but by our own power we sink like Peter. We need this Spirit of the Lord at all times, and that is why we must constantly seek his face in prayer. St. Theresa of Avila once said: „Anybody who abandons prayer does not need anybody to throw him to hell, he walks straight to hell himself." We need to pray at all times. The Lord Jesus Himself prayed constantly (cf. Mk. 1:35, Mt. 26:36-39, 44). And He passed this over to His disciples and to us through these words: „Keep watch and pray that you may not fall into temptation. The spirit is willing, but the flesh is weak" (Mt. 26:41). I believe that everyone desires holiness; we all long for holiness, our spirit is ready to walk on the path of holiness, but our flesh is not ready, it is lazy and needs to be overcome. The way to it is that which Jesus has given us: „Watch and pray". Anyone who is a nightguard or a police or a soldier knows the importance of this word "Watch". The nightguard keeps watch so that no thief or enemy will break in. The soldiers at the war front watch carefully so that the enemy will not overpower them. The Lord says: „Watch and pray", He did not just say „watch" and stop there, but „watch, and pray". Some nightguards keep watch and fall asleep sometimes. When the master of such finds them in this state, he can collect their weapons silently and walk away. The work of this kind of nightguards will come to its end, if the master is not merciful. The psalmist says „If the Lord does not keep watch, in vain does the watch man keep vigil" (Ps. 127: 1). It is the Lord who actually guards and watches. Our own job is just to go on our knees every now and then and ask Him to watch over us. When we pray, we are indirectly keeping watch, we watch and give signal to the Lord. We are just like scouters. St. Paul summarises this in his letter to the Ephesians: „Finally, build up your strength in union with the Lord and by means of his mighty power. Put on the armour that God gives you, so that you will be able to stand up against the devil's evil tricks.

For we are not fighting against human beings but against the wicked spiritual forces in the heavenly world, the rulers, authorities, and cosmic powers of the dark age. So put on God's armour now! Then when the evil day comes, you will be able to resist the enemy's attack; and after fighting to the end, you will still hold your ground. So stand ready, with truth as a belt tight round your waist, with righteousness as your breastplate, and as your shoes the readiness to announce the Good News of peace. At all times carry faith as a shield; for with it you will be able to put out all the burning arrows shot by the evil one. And accept salvation as a helmet, and the word of God as a sword which the Spirit gives you. Do all this in prayer, asking for God's help. Pray on every occasion, as the Spirit leads. For this reason keep alert and never give up; pray always for all God's people" (Eph. 6:10-18f). How do we keep alert just like St. Paul asks us to do? How can we remain awake in the Lord and not fall asleep? Praise does this wonder for us. Praise keeps us alert and sober. Praise makes us fully awake and active. Remain with the Lord and do not go away: a winner never quits and a quiter never wins! Praise the Lord and shout Halleluia to Him and the devil will run away defeated and ashamed.

2.5   Praise Makes Us Strong

Praise constitutes the core of our being. We need to praise in order to live, for without praise we become weary on our journey on earth, but with praise on our lips we shall keep our heads high and move ahead with joy. This is what gives us strength just like the Scripture puts it: ‚The joy of the Lord is your strength' (cf. Neh. 8:10). We get this joy by relying on the Lord, through praises. Heinrich Janssen also says the following concerning the wonder of praise in our lives:

„We begin to notice that the more we deep ourselves into the life of Christ, the more deeper we discover the mystery of our own life. It is then that joy will begin to well up in us. Joy leads to praises and thanksgiving. Praise in itself is the ground melody of our faith. …When the Sense of praise in our daily life becomes weaker, our faith then looses life in itself" (Translation of the German text). Praises as such perform a lot of wonders that we cannot imagine in our lives.

In praise is power
In praise is glory
In praise is strength
In praise is courage
In praise is wisdom
In praise is knowledge
In praise is healing
In praise is victory over sin and the devil
In praise is the power of God at work in us
In praise is success
In praise is peace
In praise is love

2.6   Our Miracle Begins With Praise

When we begin to praise God, His presence begins to surround us and our needs are met. Benny Hinn, a great world Evangelist of our time, attests to this fact by saying that our miracle starts at the point when we begin to bless the Lord from the depths of our soul, from all that is within us. According to him, „we need to spend time praising and worshiping God for who He is. We should be saying we praise You, Lord for shedding your blood on the cross for us, we praise You, Lord for redeeming our life, we praise You, Lord for your healing power, we praise You, Lord for your promises etc." Praise, therefore, opens the door of our miracle. We can, as such, praise God even for what we seek for, believing that it has been granted to us in faith. We can, accordingly begin to thank and glorify God for the gift of good health when we are sick, or praise Him for a good job when we seek for one, and for so many of our other needs.

2.7   Our Victory Is In Praise

A serious spiritual weapon the devil fears is praise. Francis W. Oke in his book „The Weapons of our Warfare" says in view of this: „Our warfare is not against flesh and blood, but against spiritual forces. They hate worship and praise to the most high God and are most easily routed with this weapon. Therefore, when the battle seems toughest, apply the weapon of praise. You will break the backbone of the enemy."

Jehoshaphat and his people won their battle against their enemies in praise and worship. „At the moment, they began their jubilant hymn, the Lord set ambush against the Ammonites, Moabites, and those of mount Seir who were coming against Judah; so that they were vanquished" (2 Chr. 20:22). Our victory is surely in praise. When we get ourselves deeply involved in it, the impossibility turns to be possible by the great power of God which we praise. Merlin Carothers tells us his story about his victory in praise in his book „Victory on Praise Mountain". He gives the account of how his marriage, his ministry and health were on the verge of destruction and how God gave him victory in praise. This is a great testimony to show that God is mightly present and performs wonders in praises. When you praise God, you tell God that you believe in His power; you express the fact that what you need has been granted to you already and so shall it be for you.

2.8   A Testimony Of A Young Man

A young police man once came to me telling me that he had not slept at nights for many weeks. I asked him what the problem was, but he could not tell me what exactly. I asked whether he was sick and he said no. He was just not contented with his life. And so I was moved to tell him to just go home praising and thanking God for his life and for everything around him and that he should try to make his environment good, his room should be made fine so that he will feel at home in it and that he should enjoy listening to the music of his choice and all that it takes to enjoy holy life. The young man went home and carried out the assignment, and here is his testimony: I Philip Tordue was .under great burden. Nothing was found to make my life happy. I was having sleepless nights, overthinking, depression, despiration, loneliness, etc. My life was full of trouble every corner. I was not having strength to say my prayers or to read my Bible. Even if I wanted to pray, my mind always thought of other different things. In fact, life was not easy with me for a long period of time! One day I decided to have a discussion with some Christian sisters. They then gave me some Psalms to be reading and also directed me to pay a visit to Father Theophilus at Idah Cathedral. Praise God! I visited him and we shared the word of God together. He told me to do nothing, but to keep praising the living God, and by saying thank you, Jesus, all the time. The Rev. Father also blessed some water which I took home and sprinkled in my room and burnt some insence. That very day I slept very well. Thereafter, I started experiencing some wonderful development in my life. Praise the living God! Two weeks later the D.P.O. of my Division ordered that I should be posted from Counter duty to D.C.B.'s office as I.P.0. Glory be to God! God changed my loneliness through this and replaced it with happiness in me by giving me a beautiful lady whom I intend to marry. I therefore urge you my fellow brothers and sisters in Christ to bear in mind that our God is a living God. And that wherever you go or whatever condition you find yourself in, God is always near to put you through." Praise God! This young man eventually came to introduce his beautiful fiancée to me and right before me engaged themselves by the exchange of rings. I thank God for the young man who is a happy fellow today and is now in the position to advise others on what to do in the difficult moments. I have also had encounters in my life which make me to believe that the act of thanksgiving and praise can really change situations unto good. In thanksgiving and praise one encounters divine intervention, even in difficulty.

**Thank you, Jesus!
Have you said it today?**

Chapter 3:

3.1 My Encounter With God In Thanksgiving And Praise: A Command From Above

I woke up on 8th Feb. 2001 with these words, on my lips (in German): „Lass die ganze Erde erkennen, dass der Herr Gott ist! (Let the whole earth know that the Lord is God)" (cf. 1 Kg. 8:60). It baffled me why I woke up uttering these words. But when I thought about it later, I came to a deeper insight of it. I was deeply involved in the act of thanksgiving and praise during the period I had this experience. This, therefore, made me to know exactly what the Lord was demanding of me. It is God's desire that I make people know that He is God and as such to be marvelled at, in praise and thanksgiving. In the world today many would not want to hear about God or to even recognise the fact that He exists talkless of praising Him. In such a situation, we as Christians, believers in God have to come out and tell the world that our God is really alive. We can do much through our thanksgiving and praises to Him. Our way of life has to portray the fact that God lives. We need to be people of hope and this hope we also proclaim in the act of Praise. As Christians we need to show the world that we are really redeemed. When we praise our Lord we declare that we are a redeemed people. We, therefore, need not be ashamed of proclaiming the Lord as our God and redeemer wherever we find ourselves. This is then our job to praise and proclaim the Lord as our God.

3.2   My Praise Experience In Münster

I was in Münster for my free semester in Germany. I learnt a lot of things during the period; one of the things that preoccupied my mind there was the power of praise which, like I narrated in the introduction, was enhanced by the reflections that were given by priests in the seminary where I lived. The reflections circled around the topic which was selected for that semester on the need to praise and thank God always. My stay there for a whole semester was an interesting one, but not so easy since I was faced with new challenges of a bigger institution; I was, through the power of praise, delighted in everything and was smiling around even in the face of difficulty. I was to write a term paper at a time with some German students but when I discovered that they were too slow and relaxed about it, since that was their own university and I was to finish and go back to Fulda to present my scores, I had to make up my mind to write that term paper alone within two weeks. When I started, some of my German friends doubted that I will make it within the short time. But I faced this work with determination and with praise in my heart and on my lips. I sat sometimes with my guitar to sing praises, and I finished the work within the given time - thanks to my friends who helped me to correct the work - and submitted it to the professor. I was afraid that it will not be rated good, but to my greatest surprise, the man rated my work as being a well composed and focused one and gave me a distinction. I was quite amazed at this and thanked God the more. I believe that praise gave me courage at that moment of great demand and I am happy to give the testimony today.

3.3 My Praise Experience On My Way From Münster To Fulda

My journey back to Fulda was on 20th Feb. 2001. The Lord did great wonders for me on that day. I was so worried before my departure, about how I was going to carry my luggages alone to the train station. The things I had to carry were too many that I had fear that I may not be able to carry them. I thought of dropping my guitar, but thought that if I dropped it, I would not have something to accompany my praises. As this worry was trying to overwelm me, I got up and began to sing praises and the worry disappeared. The act of praise brought the childlike faith into me. I saw my luggages piled up there, I tried to carry them, but felt pains at my back, but was not worried about that again at the moment of praising the Lord. It was at that point that a friend nocked on my door, I opened the door and saw this friend, Heiner by name. He asked me of the time of my departure, which I told him. He immediately promised that he will come and pick me to the train station with his car. As it was time, Heiner came and fulfilled his promise. He helped me to pick my bags into his car and drove me to the station. He also helped me to put everything on the train. May God bless him for his kindness! The journey began and at a point I had to change train. Before I could even come out of the train, one man already carried my big box and helped me to bring it out. God bless him too. And at the point I was to enter the other train, as I carried some of my baggages into the train, a woman just collected the rest of my luggages and brought them into the train. I was so touched that I did not even know how to express my thanks to her. The train moved on and I found myself singing praises unto the Lord for his wonderful works. I also had to change train in a town called Kassel. Before I could carry some of my bags into the train, a man, a woman and her daughter, and her daughter`s friend helped me to bring all my baggages into the train. I surprisingly saw them bringing them behind me. I was quite overwhelmed by their kind gesture! As I arrived in Fulda, I boarded a taxi. I greeted the taxi driver so friendly and asked how he was doing and he told me "schlecht". When a German says "schlecht", it means that all is not in order. There is something wrong. I asked him of the matter and he told me that his whole life is scattered. I asked further questions to know the details of the problem. He told me that he needed true love from a woman and had not found it. I told him that he needed not to be so bitter about that, and that he should rather be grateful to God for his life. He said, how could he thank God, when God does not love him. I told him to just try it and see what it would yield for him. Whether he got the point, I do not know, but we can learn from his situation that there are lots of people who have no joy of living again. That is why one hears sometimes about cases of suicide. There is something that can deliver us from this danger. That is the act of thanking God and of singing praises unto the Lord. The real life begins when one begins to sing. It is the beginning of wisdom. We only need to open our eyes and see what the Lord has done for us and be grateful to Him.

In the course of my journey from Münster to Fulda, I discovered that God actually loves me and
that He helps me through my   fellow human
beings. I just have to thank Him for his goodness
to me. Even as I approached the seminary, my fi-
nal destination, some seminarians were just waiting
at the door. They all helped me to carry my lugga-
ge to the front of the door of my room. I had earlier
worried about how I was going to open the door of
the seminary and go in, but these seminarians opened the door wide for me to go in. Praise the Lord!
Even at the front of my door, a friend of mine came
and helped me to bring everything into the room.
Another one came and asked if I was hungry,
of which I said yes, and he gave me bread and
egg. May God bless all of them for their love.
For all these things, should I not be grateful
to God? To sing the praises of God is our job,
and if we do it, we get our reward: joy, peace,
faith, strength, love, help, good health, etc.

3.4   An Experience Of God's Providence

About two weeks after my priestly ordination, my car
had an accident and was seriously damaged. When I
was taken to the scene, I stood there laughing and giving thanks to God, first of all, that nothing happened
to my cousin who was driving it when the accident
occurred. I was asked to enter the car and steer it while it was being pulled away by a towing van. While
I was in the car, I was singing praises with joy and

waving the people on the roadside with enthusiasm. Some of those people must have thought that I was not serious. I meant it all, because I knew that the Lord was going to do the best out of it, which He did. The car was taken to a panel beater who started his job and ended very well. The major problem was with the engine: we could not start the car. We tried to no avail. I brought different mechanics but nothing happened and, like a flash, came a song in Igala which I sang with faith: „Ugbo k`ona ma den, Ojo mi ach‘ ona" (my God makes a way where there is no way). I kept singing this song even as I brought in the last mechanics. They were about touching the engine to dismantle the components, when all of a sudden we heard a certain sound, as one of them tried the ignition. The car came back to life. God really makes a way where there is no way. When we affirm this in praise, He brings it to reality by making it happen.

3.5   My Entire Life Testimony

Whenever I reflect over my life, I always find a reason to say „Lord, I thank you". I am sure that my mother, father, brothers and sisters will also do the same. I, at the age of about three or four, followed my mother‘s cousin to visit my grandfather who is now late - may his gentle soul rest in peace. He lived then in a place called Emachi. I can still recall how I sat on the bar of the bicycle that was used to convey me to the village. When we arrived there, I started having a strange feeling of being totally separated from my mother and so cried to go back to her. There was no way for me to go back. I never stayed with my mother anymore as a child as from that time. I started living a new life with my grandfather and my grandmother. I could only go on holidays to see my parents once in a while. I actually longed to stay with my mother again, but it was no more possible for me. My grandfather loved me so much that he could not let me go. We often went to farm together. He gave me a yam plot to make me feel happy and fulfilled. However, I still longed to go back to my mother. I cried on the several occasions my sisters visited me. I wanted to go back with them, but destiny never allowed it again. That was how my journey towards answering God's call actually began. I had to learn to stay apart from my mother, father, brothers and sisters and to feel the pains of that separation. But I am grateful to God today for that experience. When I think about the time I spent at Emachi as a little boy, I have every reason to give thanks to God. I have every reason to feel blessed by God, because I learnt a lot from the environment and particularly from my grandfather. We later had to pack from Emachi to Ajaka. I was so happy at the thought of going to Ajaka to meet my parents, brothers and sisters. But before we could pack there my parents packed and went to Ankpa. Life at Ajaka was not an easy one; I started going to church, but was stopped after sometime by my grandfather who made me to be going to farm even on Sundays. I was not happy about it all. I reported the case to my father and he told me to be patient. I was also preparing for first Holy Communion but was not allowed to carry on the preparation. I was really not happy. I sometimes even went to the mosque with my grandfather on Sallah days. I made sure I passed through roads where I would not be seen by my Christian friends. Despite all these experiences, I had the desire of becoming a priest. I remember one day telling a school mate that I want to be a priest. My dream started becoming a reality when my grandfather called me one day and told me that I was free to continue practising my religion in good faith. He put my hands together, prayed, and slightly spat into them and closed them. I later gained admission into St. Kizito Seminary, Idah. This happened only by God's grace, because I felt that I failed the common entrance after the examination, only to be told later that my name was called in the Cathedral of Idah as one of those candidates admitted. When I went to St. Kizito, I felt I would not be able to cope with the other intelligent students, but by the special grace of God, I was able to pass all my examinations very well. And the greatest thing the Lord did for me, was the wonderful WAEC result he gave me which made it possible for me to face my call by going to the Major Seminary. I first started with spiritual year at Eruku in Kwara State (Nigeria) and later went to Makurdi in Benue State for philosophy and later to Fulda in Germany for theology. All through I had the feeling of not being capable and worthy for my call, but the grace of God made everything possible. Even at the last moment before my diaconate ordination in Fulda, I felt I would not be chosen; the same happened at my priestly ordination. It was only after the whole ceremony of my priestly ordination that it became clear to me that the Lord actually chose me to be his own servant and minister. And surprisingly enough, I was later chosen as the first parish priest of the church, where my grandfather forbade me to go to church as a child. It was unknown to the bishop that I had any connection with that church, St. Patricks Ajaka. I was filled with emotions on the day of my installation; I would have wished my dad to be there as the keys of that church, which he contributed in building and which bears his patron saint's name, where handed over to me. In all this, I have nothing to say to my God rather than to say „It is right to give you thanks and praise." I, therefore, see every reason to be grateful to God in my life daily. I believe that every individual must at least be able to find traces of God's blessings in his or her life, particularly when things are hard, and be able to give thanks.

Thank you, God!
Have you said this in the past second?

Chapter 4:

4.1   Reasons For Thanksgiving And Praise

A friend once asked me after I spoke to him over the principle of thanksgiving and praise: "How can I say ‚thank you, Jesus' every second when I am hungry?" Other questions may be: How can I thank or praise God when I am sad over the death of a dear one? How can I thank God when I am sick? These and many more such questions discourage us from saying „thank you" to God. But as we grudge over the present problems, we are breathing in the air which God provides! This may sound funny but it is the fact. If he should cease the air we are gone. So, as long as we are alive, no matter what may be our condition, let us give thanks. This can work a great wonder which we may not expect. Jesus, for example, first thanked his Father in heaven and prayed for Lazarus to come out of his grave. It was the fourth day of his burial, but the miracle happened. To God there is nothing that is impossible"(Lk.1:37). I am not asking us to now begin to expect our dear ones who died long ago to come back to life all in the name of thanking God, even though God can do all things! What I mean is that we just have to learn to thank God in all situations (cf. Eph. 5:20). If it pleases God, he will do the impossible for us, but let us just leave that to him; our own job is just to thank and praise Him, for He is our creator. That we are alive today and that Jesus has promised us eternal life is enough reason for us to thank God;

our life does not end here on earth, the perfect life which we are always longing for shall be given to us on the last day; what a great joy over the heavenly bliss which we shall enjoy at the end of time! It is already a reason for us to begin to thank God in advance. The angels and saints in heaven are already rejoicing, thanking and praising God and we shall certainly join them one day; what a great joy! St. Paul writes in his letter to the Romans: „I consider that what we suffer at this present time cannot be compared at all with the glory that is going to be revealed to us" (Rom.8:18f.). The hope for this glory gives us joy and this should lead us into thanking God. And when we also reflect on the passion of our Lord Jesus Christ we have a reason to say thank you to Jesus? It was not for his sin, but for ours, for he was without sin. He wanted us to become children of God again and that is what we are now, for we can now say „Our Father". This is enough reason to say thanks. Also the gift of the Holy Scripture which helps us on our way to heaven is a reason for us to say thanks. What have we that has not been given to us? Is it our life which we do not know how it came about? We have every cause to say „thank you, Lord" at all times, for this is our job and our duty, not because God needs it, but because we need it ourselves in order to have our way to the treasure of God's abundant blessings. And also for the Holy Spirit which God has sent to us as our helper, we need to give thanks. We have an endless list of things which we need to thank God for.

4.2 Praise God Even For Your Problems

Telling someone to praise and thank God for his problems may sound foolish at the first instance, but there lies the secret! Merlin Carothers in his famous book „Prison to praise" says out of his experience that it is when we thank God particularly for the problems we have at the moment that we get them solved. This he recommended for many, and it worked for them and many testimonies were given. This practice of thanking God for one's problems is based on what St. Paul says here: „We know that all things work for good for those who love God who are called according to his purpose" (Rom. 8:28). We are, therefore, encouraged to believe that God means the best for us, even in the worst condition. This is, therefore, the ground for thanking Him, even for our problems. Merlin emphasises the fact that it is only those who will accept the praise principle and are ready to persevere to the end that get rewarded. He describes it according to a vision he had as a ladder which is to be climbed. One climbs it in darkness until one gets to the top. Many do not have the patience and the endurance to do it, but those who persevere till the end will meet a bright light which gives joy; and to continue to have this joy, they have to keep fixing their gaze on the bright light and not on the dark cloud below them that can easily make them fall. For Merlin, according to his vision, those who fall back, discourage others by landing on them and scattering them.

When you praise the Lord, do not get discouraged at the beginning, even if nothing seems to happen, just keep on praising Him. Do not just praise Him for what you need, but praise Him for being God and keep focusing on His greatness and not on your problems.

4.3   A Testimony

I was at a point so preoccupied with the act of thanksgiving that I was so filled with joy as I thanked God almost every second that passed. Anyone around me could really see a radiation on my face, for it is a fact that when you thank or praise God that there is some special air that surrounds you! In the midst of this, I got news that my bishop called me on phone from Nigeria; I could not believe it, since I never had such calls from him in Germany. The call came a second time and the news that came from him was that my dad had passed on to Glory. I was very confused about the whole situation. I forgot about thanking God and ran out sad looking for where to find refuge. I ran to our rector and he was not there. The next place was the chapel! As I was on my way to the chapel, the thought came to me that I needed to begin to thank God for the great things he did in the life of my dad. As I started saying „thank you" to God, joy started welling up in me. I began smiling with tears. This gave me the strength to prepare for the journey home for the burial. God provided means immediately. My rector was ready to give me the assistance I needed. I booked a flight immediately and was soon on board coming home. I kept thanking God in my confusion and power kept welling up in me. As I came home, the wake-keep was already on with singing and dancing. It was a joyful moment as I stepped into our compound in the village. Someone who was observing the whole situation as I came into the house, later told me that there was a great joy around as I stepped in, and that it was as if another father of the house came in! I kept thanking God and encouraging others to do the same, and this gave us courage throughout the whole period. Even today, when I seem to feel the absence of my dad, I fill the gap with thanksgiving and I get consoled. So it is also possible to find a reason to thank God, even in the midst of sorrows. It is of paramount importance therefore, that we try and find a reason for thanking God at all times, particularly in moments of difficulty. And to do this, we must comply with certain conditions.

Chapter 5:

5. Necessary Conditions For Thanksgiving And Praise

5.1 Humility

The way we see ourselves affects our prayer to a great extent. The posture we take while praying matters much too. The recommendable posture is that of a humble servant before his master. Jesus Christ is our master, even though He is also our brother and friend. We really need to come before Him with a humble mind. The story of the samaritan and the publican in the bible is an example. The publican praised his own self-acclaimed righteousness before the Lord, but the samaritan recognised his nothingness, his dirtiness and saw how wretched he was before the Lord. He saw himself as a sinner; this pleased the Lord and his prayer was heard (cf. Lk. 18:9-14). St. Theresa of Avila described this act of humility out of her spiritual experience. She said that seeing God's holiness, she recognises her own sinfulness and dirtiness, seeing the faithfulness of God, she sees her own faithlessness. This is the right pattern of thinking before God: Thinking of His greatness and not ours and praising His goodness and not ours. It is very important for us to confess this fact, for we have all fallen short of God's grace and need his mercy. When we recognise this fact we find ourselves telling him: "Lord, have mercy on me, a sinner!"

Pope John Paul I. said that the Lord would not mind letting us to fall in weakness, in order to teach us the lesson of humility. Thus, he says: „We have to come before God with humility. When I say: 'Lord, I believe, I do not feel ashamed to feel like a child before his mother' … I will say here that I recommend just one virtue which is very dear to the Lord. He said 'learn from me, for I am humble of heart.' I will take the risk of saying something strange: 'The Lord loves humility so much that he sometimes allows grave sins. Why? Because the one who committed such a sin will become guilty and humble. No one will see himself as an angel or saint when he knows that he has done something wrong. The Lord has so much recommended that we should be humble. Even when we have done much, we are to say: 'we are unworthy slaves.' In our own case we always want to go the opposite direction, to place ourselves high, but let us remain humble, this is the christian virtue which has been given to us."

The Lord really wants us to recognise who we are and confess this fact and to stop wearing masks to pretend to be what we are not. We cannot play to be little angels when we should declare our dirtiness before the Lord. It is the man who is sick and knows and accepts the fact that he is sick, who goes to the doctor to help him. No man who goes to the doctor and tells him that he is healthy would receive any treatment from the doctor, he would only be joking. The patient has to confess what his problem is, before the doctor can know which treatment to give to him. The Lord himself says that it is the sick who needs the doctor and not the healthy and that he has come for the sinner and not for the righteous (cf. Mt. 9:12-13). He said this to the pharisees who acclaimed themselves as righteous. So, we really have to be careful. What the Lord wants from us is just the humility to accept and confess who we are: weak and not strong, sinners and not righteous, dirty and not clean enough. The psalmist says this about himself: "I was conceived a sinner, oh Lord!" (cf. Ps. 51:7). When we think like this, the Lord will really have time for us, He will then make us strong, holy and clean. It is the Lord's own work to make us strong, holy, clean and healthy and not ours to acclaim these qualities when we are actually not what we claim. If we do so, we are just like.any person putting on a mask, and thereby hiding his real identity in the public. I have come to discover that I find it difficult to praise the Lord whenever I forget to confess my nothingness before him. But the moment I say „Oh Lord, I am nothing in myself, but I praise you, for in you I find my full self, I become lighter, forget my worries and begin to give thanks and praise with all strength and joy. This shows the importance of making the confession of our humble state. Pride blocks the gate to praises, but humility opens this same gate even wider to the point that we begin to see the glory of God. We continue to see God manifesting His power in our midst so long as we remain humble. Here are the words of the Lord to us: „My son, my daughter, give glory and praise to Me. The glory and praise belong to Me and not to you. It is in not seeking glory for yourself, but for Me that you will really grow in My love and bear greater fruits which will give

Me more honour" (adapted from my personal diary). In the world, we have many temptations. Jesus Himself was tempted, so we are also not spared. We can learn a lot from the temptation of Jesus. It was temptation to misuse the power given to Him by his Father: temptation to change stone into bread because he was hungry, temptation to win the whole world through surrender to the enemy and not to His Father and the temptation to misuse the words of the scripture. These were the temptations of Jesus and we ourselves are not also safe from them today. Temptation to be great, to be regarded as the best, as the first like the apostles of Christ also had. We must consider all this as nothing. They are all passing away and anything that passes away must be considered as nothing. The worldly power is nothing, it corrupts, we must avoid it and hang on to the Lord and praise Him alone and not let ourselves become the object of praises of people. Praises belong to the Lord alone and not to us. The Lord really wants us to be humble. We can learn more about humility through the life of Christ as it is described in Phil. 2: 3ff.: „Although He was God, Christ did not count Himself equal to God ..." The glory therefore belongs to God alone and He alone must be adored and worshipped. He alone must be praised and exalted on high. The bad angel Lucifer was not ready to perform this function of giving glory to God. He rather wanted the glory for himself and that was what led to his defeat and downfall. So we have to be careful.

5.2   The Acceptance Of Oneself

Humility goes a long way in the act of accepting oneself as we were created by God. The man is happy who accepts himself as he is created by God and appreciates his entire being. I was so worried at a time about my colour and at that moment, the Lord said to me, „Theo, you have to thank me for your colour. This has brought me a great joy." I thanked the Lord for my colour, it is a gift from Him and I just have to thank Him for it. Patricia A. McLaughlin in her book „The Jesus Walk" tells a story which she heard from a priest at a retreat, in order to show the importance of seeing beauty even in one's personal life which one may think to be totally broken. It goes thus: „A priest received an exquisite Waterford crystal chalice from his parishioners. As he carried the lovely chalice to the rectory, it slipped from his hands and broke into myriad pieces at his feet. The priest marvelled at the shattered glass on the sidewalk, saying, 'How beautiful!'" Patricia commenting on this, said: „There was beauty in the brokeness of the chalice because it reflected even more light than before!" This can be applied to our individual lives, that we still appreciate and accept our lives despite some limitations. We can through this also come to forgive ourselves and others for mistakes and shortcomings of the past, which in a way will help to quicken the effect of the praises and thanks we offer to God. Patricia also related her experience about a boy named John Winter who was confined to a wheel chair because of his physical impairement.

The boy spoke with great difficulty and so hated himself at a time. He felt it was unfair for him to be in that state. He was really bitter and annoyed with God over it. It was later that he was taught in a catechism class by a sister to love one thing about himself each day. With this he can now say „I love my body!" He can even further tell himself „my body is the temple of the Holy Ghost. I give glory to God with my body. People see God in me." Some school children asked him sometime after he gave them a talk, if he would have just one wish of having a different body, and he answered: „No way! I love myself just the way I am." Once we accept ourselves, we begin to live in perpetual praise and thanksgiving to the Lord. We have every cause to praise the Lord and thank Him at every moment for who we are, what we have and for our entire destiny. We have no reasons, therefore, to be annoyed with our neighbour whose destiny we may think to be better than ours. God knows best when and what He is to give each one. He knows what is best for us. What is best for me may therefore not be the best for the other. And though we may see that not to be the best, God sees it as His best gift to us at the moment. We have no cause at all to be jealous of one another nor worry. My destiny is in the hands of God and it is quite different from that of any other person in the world. I have, therefore, no reason to be jealous of another person's destiny, because that can never be mine and mine can never be his. It is important to see ourselves and all we have as gifts from God. For all the Lord God has given us, we have the duty of giving Him thanks and praise. We show our appreciation and gratefulness through this.

5.3   The Fear Of The Lord

The word „fear" could have different meanings.
There is the fear which comes from an emotion ge-
nerated by a threatening evil. But there is another
that comes from an emotion of reverence and ve-
neration. The author of the book of‛ Proverbs must
have used the word fear in this second sense of it.
The expression "The fear of the Lord is the beginning of wisdom" (Prov. 1:7), therefore, has to do with
praising God which is an act of marvel. This passa-
ge which also appears in another form in Ps. 111:10
ends with an emphasis on the praise of God, thus:
„The root of wisdom is fear of Yahweh; those who
attain it are wise. His praise will continue for ever."
God is in himself wonderful, and so are His works.
When we discover God and His works to be wonderful, we are moved to say: „God, you are great, you are
omnipotent, you are omniscience, you are mighty etc."
We can see how we are already beginning to describe
God. We begin to praise Him through this act. We actually lack the words to use in describing God, but despite
this, we still find some fitting words to qualify Him. If
only we were able to find higher words to express the
greatness of God! What I am trying to say in essence is
that our way of describing God is limited, but despite
this limitedness we still try by all means to express it.
In doing this, we are already praising God and this
act of praising God is the beginning of wisdom.
My praising God means that I have discovered something great about God, it means that I have somehow
tasted the goodness of God. The recognition of the

greatness of the Lord is already wisdom. Who ever praises the Lord with his lips is sure to be on the path of wisdom; in fact, he already speaks the words of wisdom for the language of praise is the language of wisdom.

5.4   Believing The Lord

According to Don Moen, a famous gospel singer of our time, we can begin to thank God for the things which we have prayed for, believing that we have received them already and it shall be ours. This means that we need to thank God daily for His promises to us in the bible and by this we get these promises fulfilled in our lives. And to do this, we need to get ourselves familiar with the word of God, always reading and memorizing bible passages. We would therefore take God by His word and praise Him for it. This then expresses our trust and believe in Him. Praise in essence, therefore is the language of faith. I can for example begin to thank the Lord for His words in Mt. 8:17: „He Himself bore away our sicknesses and carried away our diseases." When I continue to thank the Lord in this way, I gradually begin to get healed. It is therefore always good to dwell on the word of God, believing in it and praising God for it.

5.5   Satisfaction With Oneself

Everyone in the world seeks happiness and satisfaction. We are searching daily without rest, and even get frustrated sometimes. Even when we have made considerable progress we are still not satisfied. We try several means through which we can actually have the peace we need, but most times to no avail. It is true that we can never have the absolute happiness and satisfaction that we long for here on earth, but we can, to a certain degree, attain or have a foretaste of this satisfaction and happiness from time to time, once we begin to take some time to reflect over life generally and discover what the world means to us, and who we are in the world, and acknowlegde and allow this fact to have an impact in our lives. I once read a book in which the author wrote on the three steps to be taken before one can become satisfied with his or her life. The steps are as follows:
-        make a reflection on death
-        peal the onion of your ego
-        ask God for what you need

I have tried these steps on certain occasions and have come to discover that they really have an effect and that they make a great impact in my spiritual life. The following wise saying was written on the gate of Apollo temple of Delphi: 'gnoti seauton' – 'know yourself'. Hans Urs von Balthasar gave his own personal interpretation to it by saying this: „Man, know that you are a human being"; but I would have it this way: „Man, know that you are a mortal being."

The human being has the temptation to always raise himself in the midst of others. Each one has this problem, pride is in each of us, this was the sin of our first parents, they wanted to raise themselves to the position of God. This is our problem in the world today, each one wants to be on the top, each country wants to be the best and number one. America wants to be at the top forever, Europe wants to be like America, and Africa would also like to rise one day and be like America. Asia would also want to be heard of in the world and Australia too. Like Lucky Dube, a Reggae musician would have it: "All are confused! The white man wants to be an African, the African wants to be like a white man and the Indian would want to be everyone." What a confusion indeed! This is what is happening to us all. We are never satisfied with who we are, what we have and with our position. If only each one were to be satisfied with his position, there would be great peace in the world. There would be no war, no hatred of any kind, all would be living like brothers and sisters! But it is a pity that each one wants to be better than the other. I, however, believe that it is not too late for us to correct ourselves, it is not too late for us to search and know who we are as human and mortal beings, who have only a few years to spend on earth and vanish. When we think about this, I think we shall at least be considerable to our neighbour in whatever we do. To consider the other and the other's need as more important, is great virtue which each of us needs to cultivate. According to Thomas a Kempis, „That man is truly great who is great in charity. He is truly great who is little in his own eyes and holdeth as naught the pinnacle of honor." (Cf. My Imitation of Christ, Bk. 1, Ch.3.).

For Thomas a Kempis, the humble knowledge of ourselves is the surer way to God than the deepest search after science. The great hindrance and trouble we have according to him is our own unmortified affection of heart and that our most important business should be to strive to overeome ourselves, and daily to gain strength over ourselves, and to grow better. For Thomas a Kempis, the highest science and most profitable lesson is to know and despise ourselves. To have a humble opinion of ourselves and to think always well and commendably of others is great wisdom and high perfection. We are struggling daily with ourselves, we want to have absolute peace, but no way, we are blocked by high opionion of ourselves, we are sad because we cannot reach what we want; we want to be at the top, but the top does not belong to us, it belongs to the Lord alone, and to Him alone must the glory and praise be given. The story of the Old Testament about the tower of Babel tells us that the people wanted to do something great and make a name for themselves. „To make a name" - this is our problem! If we would make a name for God and for our neighbour, that would be good, but we want to make name for ourselves. We really need to know who we are, like we have been advised to. And let us accept ourselves as we are, not wanting to be like God or trying to take another's position. Let us rather put God first in everything in thanksgiving and praise and in humble service of our neighbours.

5.6   Surrender

The act of surrender is somethng else that we really
have to learn and practise consciously. We cannot do
anything good without the power of God that works
in us (cf. Jn. 15:5). If this is true, we then have to
surrender all to Him totally so long as we want peace.
In order to practise the act of surrender we have to
meditate on our lives, the past and the present, and
see where the hands of God helped us. This will
help us further to go into praises and thanksgiving. When we count the blessings of the Lord in
our lives, we are overwhelmed. We are then moved to entrust our future into the hands of the Lord.
The battle is the Lord's and not ours, so we have to
surrender it all to Him. The act of surrender can go
a long way. When we think of the people God has
blessed us with, we are moved to praise Him for
their lives. We do not just stop there, we need to
also surrender them into His hands for protection.
I should be able to say: Lord, I thank you for
my father Patrick and for my mother Janet and
I surrender them to You for Your blessings.
I thank You for my brothers and sisters and I surrender them to You to be blessed by You. I thank
You for my uncles and aunties and all my rela-
tions, friends, benefactors and benefactresses and
I surrender them all to You for Your blessings.
This list could continue a long way, so long as we
have something or someone to thank God for.

5.7 Dependence On The Holy Spirit

The Holy Spirit is our helper and advocate. We also need to surrender all to Him, and entrust our lives daily to Him. There are so many things we embark on, which do not seem to be fruitful, we have to surrender all these to the Holy Spirit, who helps us in all our ways. He often waits for us to say: I surrender all to you. Let us try this and see the amount of peace that we shall enjoy. We need the support of the Holy Spirit to praise and thank the Lord. We have no strength on our own to praise God, it comes also from God Himself in the Holy Spirit. So to really live a life of praises and thanksgiving we have to dwell in the Holy Spirit. He must be our friend and our helper in the act of praise and thanksgiving. When we live and commune with the Holy Spirit, praises and thanksgiving flow naturally from us. We would no longer have the need to force it out of ourselves, it comes on its own. The Holy Spirit helps us also in so many other ways. He helps us to love, and to know and proclaim the word of God. He gives us power to do all these things and many more. He helps us to bear good fruits, that will last forever. What is that difficulty that we have? Let us bring it to the Holy Spirit and see the great joy that we shall experience, and out of this joy shall come praises and thanksgiving.

5.8   Counting Your Blessings

As a popular Chorus says it:
Count your blessings, name them one by one
Count your blessings, see what the Lord has done
Count your blessings, name them one by one
And it will surprise you what the Lord has done!
This is a song I love singing. It is really a great
hymn which inspires us to give thanks and praise
to the Lord. In the Old Testament, Sarah the wife
of Abraham, counted her blessings and gave praise to God (cf. Gen. 21:6). The sons and the daugh-
ters of Israel counted their blessings after their ex-
odus from Egypt and they sang praises to the Lord
(cf. Ex. 15). The prophet Daniel counted the Lord's
blessings on him and he gave praise to the Lord (cf.
Dan. 9:4). The Blessed Virgin Mary counted her blessings and gave praise to the Lord (cf. Lk.1:46- 55).
Zacharia counted his blessings as God blessed him
and his wife Elizabeth with a child (John the Bap-
tist) in their old age and he gave praise to the
Lord as he sang the Benedictus (cf. Lk. 1:68-79).
Benedictus means blessing. This means that he sang
over the Lord's blessings on him and gave glory to
God. If we want, we can continue to make a longer
list of those who counted their blessings and gave
praise to the Lord. We too can count the Lord´s blessings on us at each moment of our lives and give praise to the Lord and let His bright light shine on us.
It is really a sweet activity to count one's blessings
and to give praise to the Lord. It heals, strengthens,
motivates and encourages us on our journey towards

God. It brightens our lives, gives us joy, peace and satisfaction. It manifests the glory of the Lord in and through us, it is a holy and joyous activity. It drives away the darkness of sin and sadness, it liberates and loses us from the bonds of gloominess, weariness, tiredness, depression, and above all, it increases our faith and promotes love, hope and charity in us.

5.9   Rejoicing Always

St. Paul in his letter to the Philipians encouraged them to rejoice always (cf. Phil. 4:4). St. Paul gave this encouragement because he knew the enemies' tactics against God's children, which is to make them sad. And when they are sad he tries to take the upper hand by leading them into depression. It is against such tactics that St. Paul launched this attack by telling the faithful people to "Rejoice". Whether you like it or not, the enemy must use his trick on you at each moment of the day, but once you refuse to be sad by rejoicing in the Lord, he becomes terribly disappointed. In the book of Nehemiah, the people were told not to mourn, but to allow the joy of the Lord to be their strength (cf. Neh. 8:10). When you have the joy of the Lord in you, worries will have no space in you, you will be happy and the devil will be sad. So rejoice in the Lord always and sing praises to God with thanksgiving in your heart and you are a conqueror. Sing and play music in your heart to the Lord, always giving thanks for everything to God the Father in the name of our Lord Jesus Christ (Eph. 5:19-20).

„Anyone who thanks God from his heart will become rich in himself."
(Albert Schweitzer)

APPENDIX

I.   A Prayer of Praise

Lord, you have blessed me with the gift of life and I praise you. You have blessed me with the gift of Yourself in Jesus Christ and in the Holy Spirit and I give You thanks and praise. Lord, You have blessed me with your Mother, the blessed Virgin Mary, who prays for me and for all Your children all over the world, and I give You glory and praise. Lord, You have blessed me with countless number of people and with so many blessings I cannot finish counting. I bless and glorify You for all Your goodness and love. I bless Your holy name. You are God forever, Your glory shines above the skies and Your love abides with us forever. Lord, be exaulted above the heavens, let Your glory be above all the earth.

(Out of my private journal).

II.   A Hymn of Thanksgiving

Give thanks to Yahweh for He is good,
for His faithful love endures forever.
Give thanks to the God of gods,
for his faithful love endures forever.
Give thanks to the Lord of lords,
for His faithful love endures forever. (Ps. 136., 1-3)

III.   A Prayer of Praise (2)

The Lord is great and worthy to be praised. His love endures forever, let everyone who lives give praise to the Lord, let every living thing give praise to the Lord. The Lord manifests His power in our praises. Oh what a great miracle! That we sinners could be pleasing to God! This is really the great miracle that praises do in our lives. My soul magnifies the Lord, my spirit rejoices in God, my saviour. He has done great wonders in my life and holy is His name forever. Adonai is His name. He is the mighty warrior in battle. He is the great God of our lives. He needs to be praised and glorified. Oh what a great gift for us! To sing praises unto the Lord and to please the Lord in our own way! The Lord is really great and powerful. Jahweh is His name. The Lord is mighty and excellent. His power fills the whole earth. His love lasts forever. Let us rejoice in the Lord and sing praises unto His name, for the Lord is God forever. He is our creator. He formed us and brought us to life. He is our God who saves us from all evils. He delivers us from so many dangerous forces in the world. Let us give Him praise and thanks, for He is our God forever. He is our God who answers by fire. He sends His Spirit into the world and renews the surface of the earth. God is good and worthy of our praises. Let the heavens and the earth and all things that live on it give praise and thanks to the Lord. The Lord is great. He is mighty in battle. He is the Lord of life. He is the giver of life. He is in charge of our lives. He is the author of the whole of creation. Lord is His name. Amen. **(Out of my private journal).**

IV.   Prayer of Thanksgiving

My Lord, thank You for saving my life.
Thank You for delivering me from death.
Thank You for bringing me back to life.
I will live to praise You all my life.
I will live to give You glory, and to give You honour all my life.
You are God forever.
You are rny saviour forever.
You are my protector forever.
You are my companion forever.
Give praise to the Lord, exhalt His name forever, for He has redeemed me from the net of the evil ones.
He has made me to live again, to see the light of the day, and I praise Him.
He is my God forever.
Lord is His name.
He has power over the heavens and the earth to do whatever He wills.
He has power to take life away and to bring it back.
He is the author of creation and of my life, the owner of my life and the life of every being on earth.
All life belongs to the Lord. He does with it whatever He wants. May His name be praised and glorified both now and forever. Amen.
Sing and give praise to the Lord at all times,
for He has redeemed you from death.
He will keep watch over you wherever you go and will never let the hands of the enemy touch you. Lord Almighty is His name. Alleluia!
(Out of my private journal).

V. Prayer of Praise

The Lord is a mighty God.
He is my God who stays with me wherever I go.
He is my Lord and my God.
May His name be praised both now and forever.
The power of the Lord is great.
The power of the Lord is everlasting.
His goodness lasts from age to age.
His love endures forever.
He loves us despite our sins.
He is God forever.
He is compassionate and kind.
May His name be praised both now and forever.
May all creation shout and praise His name.
Lord is His name and He is the ruler over all the earth.
He is the God of Israel, the God of Abraham, Isaac and Jacob and He is my own God and the God of all creation both now and forever. Amen.
(Out of my private journal).

VI. Prayer of praise

Oh God, You are worthy to be praised.
You are God forever.
You do wonders for Your servants.
Your servants are happy because of Your great deeds and love for them.
You are mighty, You are holy.
You are great, You are the king of kings, the Lord of

lords. You are God with us, the Emmanuel, the conqueror in battle.

The great I am, the most high God, the blessed and holy one of Israel.

May Your name be praised and glorified above the heavens and on earth forever and ever.

(Out of my private journal).

VII.   An Invitation to praise

Sing, all creation, sing to God in gladness!
Joyously serve Him, singing hymns of homage!
Chanting His praises, come before His presence!
Praise the Almighty! Know that our God is Lord of all ages! He is our maker; we are all His creatures!
People He fashioned, sheep He leads to pasture!
Praise the Almighty! Great in His goodness is the Lord we worship; Steadfast His kindness, love that knows no ending! Faithful His word is, changeless, everlasting! Praise the Almighty!
(A Hymn from the appendix, for the season in the divine Office. Sat. Week 4).

VIII.   Praise of the Lord, our creator

It is good to give thanks to the Lord, to make music to Your Name, 0h Most High, to proclaim Your love in the morning and Your truth in the watches of the night, on the ten-stringed lyre and the lute, with the murmuring sound of the harp.

Your deeds, Oh Lord, have made me glad, for the work of Your hands I shout with joy. Oh Lord, how great are Your works! How deep are your designs! The foolish man cannot know this! And the fool cannot understand.

Though the wicked spring up like grass and all who do evil thrive, they are doomed to be eternally destroyed.

But You, Lord, are eternally on high. See how Your enemies perish, all doers of evil are scattered.

To me you give the wild-ox's strength. You anoint me with the purest oil. My eyes look in triumph on my foes. My ears heard gladly of their fall.

The just will flourish like the palm-tree and grow like a Lebanon cedar.

Planted in the house of the Lord they will flourish in the courts of our God, still bearing fruits when they are old, still full of sap, still green, to proclaim that the Lord is just.

In Him, my rock, there is no wrong. (Ps.92)

IX.   The Majesty Of God And The Dignity Of Man

How great is Your Name, Oh Lord, our God, through all the earth!

Your majesty is praised above the heavens, on the lips of children and of babes.

You have found praise to foil Your enemy, to silence the foe and the rebel.

When I see the heavens, the work of Your hands, the

moon and the stars which You arranged, what is man that You should keep him in mind, mortal man that You care for him?

Yet You have made him little less than a god. With glory and honour you crowned him, gave him power over the works of Your hand, put all things under his feet. Yes, even the savage beast, birds of the air and fish that make their way through the waters.

How great is Your name, O Lord, our God, through all the earth! **(PS. 8).**

X.   Prayer of Total Trust

Jesus, my help comes from You alone
I cannot stop sinning unless You help me
My becoming holy comes from Your hands
My healing comes from Your hands
My happiness and joy come from Your hands
Oh Jesus, save me, for without You I am lost
Oh Jesus, I need You
My salvation comes from Your hands
My becoming a new man comes from Your hands
My success comes from Your hands
Oh Jesus, without You I can do nothing
You are all to me
You are the way for me
You are the truth that I seek
You are the life that I desire,
You are the love that I long for
You are the satisfaction that I need
You are the peace that I look for

You are the power that I want to possess

You are the absolute wisdom that I love

Jesus, You are the only one who can change me from the old man that I have been to a new young man

You are the only one who can transform my life into a living spring of love for humanity

You are the only one who can help me to control my desires

You are the only one who can change me from the sinner that I am into a saint

You are the only one who can make me a conqueror and a victor over my life

You are the only one who can change me from the proud man I have been into a humble man

You are the only one who can change me from the liar that I have been into a man of truth

Oh Jesus, You are the only one who can change me from the dead man I have been into a living man

You are the only one who can change my darkness into light

You are the only one who can transform my sadnes into joy

You are the only one who can make me a happy man

Oh, my Jesus, all power belongs to You

You are rissen indeed and You live forever and ever

I get to know You daily more and more through Your wonderful works

You are the only one who can save us

You have saved us from sin and death

You are the only one who can deliver us from the punishment we deserve for our sins

Jesus, You are the word of God, You are the object of

my admiration
I give You glory and praises now and forever
You are the conqueror, who has won the battle for us
Help us to claim Your victory
You have overcome sin and death our worst enemies
Have mercy on us
You are the most high God
You are the one who changed the harlot
Mary Magdalene into a saint
You brought Lazarus back to life
You changed St. Paul who was an enemy into a good friend and a soldier of Christianity
You changed St. Augustine who was a great sinner to a holy man
You have done great wonders, uncountable wonders in the history of humanity
Jesus, have mercy on me and make it my turn today
Change me a sinner this day into your own instrument of love
Change my ignorance into your own wisdom and love
Change me, a man of fears, into a courageous man and fill me with the Holy Spirit
Change me a glutton into a man of abstinence
Change me, a man of avarice, into a man of charity and love
Change me a man of lustful desires into a man of purity
Lord Jesus, I trust in You, I believe that You can change me and that You have already started it
I will live to sing Your praises from Your altar all the days of my life

I will live to proclaim Your good deeds to me and to humanity all the days of my life

This day is the day of my salvation

You are with me here and I give You glory

My Jesus, I love You, have mercy on me

My Jesus, I need You

Have mercy on me

My Jesus, I trust in You and in Your love for me

Have mercy on me

My Jesus, You are here with me now and all the days of my life

Have mercy on me

Yours I am and Yours I remain forever, do with me whatever You will and take the glory

I can see You holding my hands now, my Lord Jesus

I can see You leading me to victory

Jesus, I can see You making me a happy man

I can see You making me a healthy man

I can see You taking my sins away

I can see You transforming my life and making it into a spring of life and love for my neighbours

I can see You making me holy

I can see You leading me to serve You

I can see You saving me from all dangerous situations

I can see You holding my hands now

I can see You carrying me in Your arms now

I can see You making me to smile now

I can see You washing me clean from my sins and guilts now

I can see You blessing me with Your love, your wisdom and eloquence now

I can see You making me intelligent now

I can see You making me a humble man now

I can see You making me a man of love and charity now

I can see You making me a courageous man now

I can see You visiting me now

I can see You comforting me now

I can see You transforming my family into a home of love, peace and joy

I can see You protecting me from my enemies

I can see You granting me success in all my endeavours

I can see You leading me to greater heights

I can see You teaching me Your wisdom

I can see You teaching me how to talk

I can see You teaching me how to be kind

I can see You making me a man of faith

I can see You giving me the strength and the grace I need to work hard

I can see You touching people's lives through me

I can see You preaching Your word through my tongue and through my actions and thoughts

I can see You blessing me with Your Holy Spirit and with all His gifts

I can see You smiling at me

I can see You showing me Your love

I can see You lifting me up from my worries and sorrows

I can see You all over wherever I go

We are forever together, Oh, my good and loving Jesus. It is right to give You thanks and praise

May Your name be praised forever and ever. Amen.

(Modified out of my private journal)

XI.   Prayer of Confidence

The Lord is my shepherd
There is nothing I shall want
Fresh and green are the pastures
Where He gives me repose
Near restful waters He leads me
To revive my drooping spirit
He guides me along the right path
He is true to His name
If I should walk in the valley of death
No evil would I fear
For You are there with Your rod and staff
With this You give me comfort
You prepared a banquet for me in the sight of my
foes
My head You have anointed with oil
My cup is overflowing
Surely goodness and mercy shall follow me all the
days of my life
In the Lord's own house shall I dwell
Forever and ever. Amen.
(Ps., 23).

XII.   A hymn of thanksgiving

Thank You for giving me the morning
Thank You for ev'ry day that's new
Thank You I can know my worries
Can be cast on You
Thank You for all my friends and brothers

Thank You for all the men that live
Thank You for even greatest enemies
I can forgive
Thank You I have my occupation
Thank You for ev'ry pleasure small
Thank You for music, light and gladness
Thank You for them all
Thank You for many little sorrows
Thank You for every kindly word
Thank You for everywhere Your guidance
Reaches every land
Thank You for I see Your word has meaning
Thank You for I know Your spirit here
Thank You because You love all people
Those both far and near
Thank You, Oh Lord, You spoke unto us
Thank You for our words You care
Thank You, Oh Lord, You came among us
Bread and wine to share
Thank You, Oh Lord, Your love is boundless
Thank You that I am full of You
Thank You, You made me feel so glad
And thankful as I do
(Taken from Catholic hymn book, published in Ibadan,
Nigeria, 1976. This hymn can help us to get into the
mood of thanksgiving. I always enjoyed it whenever
we sang it in those days as minor seminarians. I never
really knew its importance as at that time, but today I am
very grateful to the man or woman who composed it.)

XIII   The Magnificat (Song of Praise) of Mary, Mother of Jesus

My soul glorifies the Lord
My spirit rejoices in God my saviour
He looks on His servant in her lowliness
Henceforth all ages will call me blessed
The Almighty works marvels for me
Holy is His name
His mercy is from age to age
On those who fear Him
He puts forth His arm in strength
And scatters the proud-hearted
He casts the mighty from their thrones
And raises the lowly
He fills the starving with good things
Sends the rich away empty
He protects Israel, His servant,
Remembering His mercy The mercy promised to our
fathers To Abraham and his sons for ever
(Lk. 1, 46 – 55).

I will give thanks to You with all my
heart, Oh Lord,
for You have answered me
(Ps. 137:1).

ABBREVIATIONS

C.A.N.	Christian Association of Nigeria
CCC	The Catechism of the Catholic Church
Cf.	Compare
D.C.B.	Divisional Crime Branch
D.P.O.	Divisional Police Officer
Etc.	et cetera – and so on
I.P.O.	Investigation Police Officer
W.A.E.C.	West African Examinational Council

BIBLIOGRAPHY

Carothers, M., Victory on Praise Mountain, word of faith Publications, Benin-City, Nigeria, 1979.

Carothers, M., Prison to Praise, Logos International, Plainfield, New Jersey, 1970.

Dziewas, D., Ein Kleines Buch der Dankbarkeit, Oncken Verlag, Kassel, Germany, 2000.

Egbunu, E. F., Get your Prayers Answered by Praying in the Spirit, Spiritual Warfare Apostolate Publications (SWAP), Idah, Nigeria, 1999.

Gorman J. J., My Imitation Of Christ by Thomas a Kempis, Ibadan, Nigeria, 1982.

Gossett, D., There's Dynamite in Praise, Ben Publishing, Secunderbad, Andhra Pradesh, India, 1974.

Hinn, B., Lord, I Need A Miracle, Thomas Nelson Inc., Publishers, Nashville, Tennessee, 1982.

Kwazu, F. C. B., How To Carry Your Cross, Snaap Press, Enugu, Nigeria, 2003.

McLaughlin, P. A., The Jesus Walk, The Road to Healing Body and Soul, St. Pauls, Bandra, Mumbai, 1998.

Oke, F. W., The Weapons of our Warfare, Highland, Guildford, Surrey, 1994.

Okenyi, M. E., Prayer is Power. The Secret of Answered Prayer, Enugu, Nigeria, 2003.

Peale, N. V., How to be your best. A Treasury of practical Ideas, Gospel Press & Literature International, Benin City, Nigeria, (Date not given).

The Catechism Of The Catholic Church, Paulines Publications Africa, Kenya, 1994.